The Desk Was Already Here

SHAMON LAWRENCE

UBUNTU
BOOKS

NEW YORK

Published in the United States by Ubuntu Books, an imprint legacy of witness, remembrance, and return.

Ubuntu Books is driven by a passion for community-rooted, conviction-driven literature.

Some titles, lines, and references throughout this collection are drawn from or inspired by the works of Langston Hughes, Countee Cullen and fall under fair use for transformative and critical purposes.

This is a work of creative nonfiction. While the events are often based on the author's real experiences, some names, characters, and identifying details have been changed or composited for privacy and literary purposes. Any resemblance to actual persons, living or dead, is purely coincidental.

Typeset in Bakersville, Garamond, and Viner Hand ITC.

Scripture quotations taken from The Holy Bible, New International Version®, NIV®. Copyright © 1973, 1978, 1984, 2011 by Biblica, Inc. Used with permission of Zondervan. All rights reserved worldwide. www.zondervan.com

ISBN 979-8-218-71482-6

Interior layout and design by Ubuntu Books. Cover art sketched and envisioned by the author, rendered with the assistance of generative intelligence tools.

Printed in the United States of America.

For the ones who sat before me—

in desks that creaked, collapsed, or never quite fit.

For the ones who taught me—

without knowing they were teaching.

For the boy I was,

for the teacher I became,

and for the desk that was already here.

"Yet do I marvel at this curious thing:
To make a poet Black, and bid him sing."
—Countee Cullen, Yet Do I Marvel

"Then the LORD reached out his hand and touched my
mouth and said to me, "I have put my words in your mouth."
—Jeremiah 1:9 (NIV)

"Go home and write a page tonight."
—Langston Hughes, Theme for English B

THE CONTENTS

Prologue   The Call...................................... 1

The Placement   The Desk Was Already Here......................... 5

The Story Continued.............................. 6

The Day Amnesia Swept the School.................. 7

The Silence Was Me.............................. 9

The Desk Thirsts................................ 1

The Witness   "Uncle Law..................................... 1

Their Desk is Not Our Desk........................ 1

Archive Notice................................. 1

Fire Drill..................................... 1

The Bell...................................... 1

"Did You Forget?".............................. 2

You Were Already Here.......................... 2

The Response   A Desk Rolls Through New York.................... 2

Theme for Writing II............................ 2

Letter to Countee.............................. 2

The Reconstruction   Lemon Loaf................................... 3

"Shamon Q. Lawrence"........................... 3

If You Remember Me............................ 3

Notes   Notes on the Poems............................. 3

THE CALL

"To make a poet Black, and bid him sing."
– Countee Cullen

I did not set out to write this book. I was, at first, only trying to make sense of where I'd been placed: a desk in a classroom where I was no longer a student, but something else—part teacher. Part watchman. All witness.

The desk became a symbol long before I recognized it as one. In school, I sat in a desk that rocked slightly on one, or two, uneven legs. Placed. Still. Compliant. Years later, I returned to a desk— not as a student, but as an educator. And it looked the same. Same laminate top, same metal frame, same weight. But now, I wasn't the one being taught—at least not officially. I was the one expected to teach, to lead, to protect. The desk remained unchanged. As you'll discover, I cannot say the same for myself.

This book is about that transformation. It's about inheritance. Not solely the legacy of education in this country, but what it means to inherit a role, a system, a position that carries with it history and harm. I began writing these poems when I realized I had not just walked into a classroom. I had stepped into a story already in motion. The desk was already here. It carried the marks of who came before: silenced students, overlooked brilliance, deferred dreams.

It was Cullen who named the paradox first: "To make a poet Black, and bid him sing." That line follows me through lecture halls, subway platforms, office hours, staff meetings, and restless nights. This glorious curse carries its own proof. It observes the tension: that to be Black, to be a poet, to be called to speak beauty into a system built on silence—is a calling filled with contradiction. Still, the bidding calls.

Langston Hughes, too, heard that bidding. You can hear it in his lecture notes, in the boldness of "Theme for English B," in the way he carved space in a world that never made room. Both he and Cullen walked the streets I walked. They studied blocks from where I taught. I carry the same discourse. The same desire to restore the old wells.

"Isaac reopened the wells that had been dug in the time of his father Abraham, which the Philistines had stopped up after Abraham died, and he gave them the same names his father had given them."
—Genesis 26:18 (KJV)

They wrote into a world that refused to see them fully, and they sang anyway.

I don't pretend to write as their contemporaries, or merely in their shadow. I write in response. I dig.

This collection is a meditation written on the sacred desk. The weight, the promise, the permanence. Some poems are quiet reflections—others, are fragments of memory. A few speak directly to desks where my presence lingers long after the last dismissal. Where I was is where I'll always be. So, fret not, descendants. Sit at what remains of this desk. We are part of the same story: one Black man's attempt to make sense of the position he inherited, and the legacy he hopes to leave behind.

There is no easy arc here. But if a throughline exists, it is this: I was bid to sing. And this book is the sound that followed.

THE
PLACEMENT

The Desk Was Already Here

The desk stands on this pillar,
 a memory of ancient ruins
hinged on eternity's heartbeat.
Its legs dig deep past linoleum,
past concrete and bedrock, into something
older
than curriculum.

It was not made by hands.
No one remembers its origin.
It was here before fire drills.
Before rubrics.
Before the first roll.

The desk desires nothing
but to witness.

Holding the memories of chalk,
the muffled slam of a bookbag
dropped in frustration,
the pencil-tip snapped in silence—
the desk is older than the school.
Older than the man who named the street.
Older than the city's zoning lines.

It is primordial, still.
Watching the teacher
try to fill time
with something

worth remembering.

The Story Continued

I sat near the window
where brown paper muted the sun—
taped at the corners,
still curling like it wanted out.
A fix so fragile,
that upon lift, lets that bright,
dusty air in.

We'd read a passage aloud
and in the silence after,
I saw the shadows
not in the margins,
but in the light
slipping through the taped seams.

My eyes wandered,
not to leave the story
but to see it continue
past the page.
I traced her
through the gap in the paper seam,
into the hallway,
past the lockers,
into somewhere the bell couldn't follow.

The Day Amnesia Swept the School

That morning,
Davonte walked through the front doors
like a sunbeam vertically fixed in fresh Jordans.
Won the science award.
Laughed at the assistant principal's joke.

He scored a 97 on his math test.
Held the door for a teacher carrying test
booklets.
Recommended Hamlet
to his classmate in the lunch line.

They said he was going places.
They said he made the school look good.
They clapped for him in two languages. Maybe
three.

But at precisely 2:07 p.m.,
Amnesia swept her brow.
She tiptoed into the main office and
cracked her knuckles over the PA system.
She whispered softly to every soul:

"Forget."

Forget the certificate.
Forget the A.
Forget the smile, the posture, the poems.

And they did.

Now he was just
another body in Room 217.

Detention.
No trial.
No logic.

Just a laminated sheet
and a staff member who refused
to make eye contact.

He cried.
And no one noticed.
Or maybe we did—
I mean, they did,
but thought it was part of the script.

Me—
I stood at the doorway
holding the award I'd once announced,
its gold seal now dissolving in my sweaty palms,
like it belonged to a version of him
I never quite met.

I opened my mouth to speak
but found nothing

nothing to undo,
nothing to remember, that
forgetting hadn't already snatched.

The Elephant in the Classroom

I taught you too soon
to survive this design—
to shrink yourself
into its symmetry.
To sit still.
To not speak
unless asked.

I called it care.
I called it love,
when I meant fear.
I told you
stay in line
as if the line led home.

You raised your hand.
I praised structure.
Feared your spark.
Flinched
when you questioned the task.
Lowered your voice
with a rubric.

You asked
can we rest
and I spoke
God help me
rigor will make you free.

But it didn't.
It made you disappear
in plain sight.

I watched you go still
while the scopes marched on
and on.

That silence—

that was me.

The Desk Thirsts

They say it's just laminate
and rusted metal,
but I've heard it thirst.

It swallowed the hall pass whole.
Chewed a name-sized void into a referral.

I hear it hum when the room is quiet
A soft remembering.

One leg shorter than the rest
so, it rocks,
just enough to remind you:

I'm alive.

I saw a boy tap it once,
barely…
his name disappeared
from roll.

The desk has a mouth.
And it speaks.

THE
WITNESS

"Uncle Law"

As difficult as it is
to spot the first popping kernel,
so, it was with the name.

I never asked for it.
Didn't expect it.
Wasn't sure who said it first.

But one day,
a girl in the second row
called out,
"Uncle Law, you ever went to Jamaica?"
like it had always been my name.

And it stuck.

Not the sticky kind
that mocks,
but the sacred kind
that sees.

It wasn't "Mr."
or "Sir."
It wasn't what they called
anyone else.

It was what you call someone
who reminds you
of whom raised you.

Who shows up
and laughs
and teaches you how to stay soft
without breaking.

Some teachers get respect.
Others get silence.
I got family.

Not always.
Not from everyone.
But enough.

And on the days
when the desk gnawed its teeth,
and my lesson fell flat,
and the printer jammed again,
All I desired to hear was,
"Uncle Law, read mine first?"

to remind me—

this room
was never just—

mine.

Their Desk is Not Our Desk

From here
I imagine the growl strains his throat—
but the preacher persists,
tugging syllables from above
and embedding them deep in
the lungs of glory.

Deacons fan themselves
like they're beating back Hell's gates,
and a Sister waves her hand
before the Spirit even lands.

Peppermints pop
between responses and sighs—
sugary shells cracking like a mighty fire.
A quiet sweetness, a memory,
in a room that demands all.

I sat a few pews back,
shirt tucked, shoes I'll grow into,
watching the Word
fall like sweat
from his brow
to the wood of his desk—
sturdy, sacred,
holding some truth.

And I wonder now,
in rooms where desks are metal and gum-stuck,

who decided what kind of weight
a desk should carry.

Even then,
before I knew the shape of praise,
I knew this was a kind of power
that didn't need to explain itself.

It just thundered,
and we said Amen.

And still,
I sit at other desks
too narrow for a full breath,
etched with names
that never made the program.

No thunder here.
Only the scrape
of chairs and tests.
Only the weight.

Archive Notice

on the first day of school

Do not add me to the archive.

I am not the subject,

I am the witness.

Let me live in your present tense,
not your cabinet.

Fire Drill

There are
drawings

in my desk:

notes

folded
like

birds,

smiles

in
crayon,
dreams on
wide-ruled
paper.
If the room burned,
I wouldn't seek the exit.
I'd run to save the true record.

The Bell

No
it wasn't the bell.
It was the hush that followed it.
How thirty bodies became a single breath
a moment that listened back.

"Did You Forget?"

A student asked me once.
That's all.
But the question grew legs.
It follows me now.
Even on weekends.

You Were Already Here

You never asked to speak.
Didn't raise your hand.
Didn't even sit in your assigned seat.

But somehow this room knew you.
The light bent around the corners of your face
like it had practice.

I saw you beside the radiator,
hood up,
writing a name
you weren't ready to say out loud.

You never said a word that day.
But something in me
marked you present anyway.

A Desk Rolls Through New York

Cherubs pour gourds of light
into this tall glass box.

Fluorescents hum overhead.
Light bounces off white walls
and purple banners
that sag from past glory.

The Empire State Building stands guard.
Proctoring, judging.

Final exam.
British Literature.
I had not slept,
but I had prepared.
And my pen
pressed down like prophecy.

"Analyze the voice," they said.

I looked around
to find a sea of bowed heads,
hoodies up,
sleeves rolled,
earbuds in,
phones tucked just out of view.

Blake walked through London.

I sat in my desk
and rolled
half an inch forward.

But it was enough
to tilt the world.

My chair creaked
like it had something to say.
The rubber wheels snagged
on the past.

My elbow hit the plastic armrest,
etched with someone else's initials.
The desk whispered,
You're not the first to see.

And I saw it:

New York
        dreams
                in bulk.

I passed the exam.
But I remember
none of the answers.

Only the silence,
the light,
and the feeling
of being moved

by something
that couldn't move at all.

Alas, a miracle—
that in a room this bright,
with a desk this old,
you need not leave
to arrive.

Theme for Writing II
after Hughes

We met in Weinstein Hall's
basement lair
where the professor spoke
like he was
delivering an oft-recited ghost elegy.

The room felt like a half-written prompt.

NYU, 2019.
Writing II.

Our theme?
Migrants, migrant writing,
what it means to be
from somewhere
and nowhere at once.

There were seventeen of us.
Only one of me.

The boy with the stiff collar
wrote about border patrol
as metaphor.
The girl beside me
linked migration to her grandmother's arthritis.
I said little.
Listened.

The walls were pale yellow.
One window.
Creaking pipes
above our heads like distant thunder.

We studied movement.
I kept still.
But something in me
was already packing a bag.
Some ancestral hunger
pressing up against the zipper seams.

The professor wrote the word:
Displacement
on the board like it was
his mother's maiden name.

I didn't know the assignment.
But I wrote anyway.
Each line a migration of its own,
separated at birth,
carving, in ink, a place
in this far white terrain.

This is my theme:
I've crossed no borders,
but my soul migrates
down my forearm to grip the pen

Ethereal consternation writes
something that could pass

for scholarship.

I left that class
with one essay,
a quiet ache,
and the knowledge
that some of us are always writing
from beyond.

Letter to Countee
after "Yet Do I Marvel"

I've sat at desks that creaked like pews,
annotated scripture in margins,
taught students who use psalms as expletives,
scratched on the backs of detention slips.

You asked why God made you Black and bid
you to sing.
I was not asked.
I was summoned.

Your question became my inheritance.
A throatful of splinters I mistake for melody.

Sometimes I teach in classrooms
where the walls listen more,
where the floor holds secrets,
where a child's silence is mistaken
for defiance.

I watch the light from the Smart Board
paint the crown of a boy who just learned
of petition, plea,
and still, no one sees him.

I carry the burden of words.
But my eyes see more,
and my ears hear more—
than my pen can claw to this page.

But I write anyway
with chalk and ache,
on the backs of call slips,
in the hollows of their names.

And when I cannot sing,
I hum.
And when I cannot hum,
I hold their breath for them.
I write them a future
in an undecipherable cursive.

Still marveling,

—Shamon

THE
RECONSTRUCTION

Lemon Loaf

I could not rush up the rugged stairs
under the corner of W 4th
& Washington Square East any faster.

My brain outruns my feet—shame, my ego.
Soon, I forget the page and search for a poem.

The smell of mothballs
and lemon-iced cake
rises like old hymns.

A folding chair scrapes back.
An uncle says grace.
And just like that,
I am ten again.

The smell of sugar, starch, fellowship.
A room where I ate more than what
once consumed me.

The barista shouts "Shamon,"
But I'm still bowed
in a forgotten childhood prayer.

Shamon Q. Lawrence
after the name on the desk

The school's gossip remains steady
as she begins tapping.
The nameplate—mine—
becomes her drumstick.
She doesn't notice the way
it rings.

Another twirls it above her head,
absentminded,
as if flagging down a memory.

They take it, pass it,
press it into the desk's skin.
Smudge it with notes,
graze it mid-whispered gossip.
Not once do I stop them.

I watch them repurpose my name
like chalk, like slang,
like something that belonged to them first.
Some days they flip it backward.
Some days they forget it's there—
but never move it far.

Something about this desk.
Something about my name on this desk.
It holds their noise
without cracking.

And when the room empties,
I find it back in place,
always slightly off-center.
As if the desk knows
I never quite sat still either.

If You Remember Me
for my professor

"I wonder if it's that simple?"
—Langston Hughes, Theme for English B

You didn't tell me to write a page.
You asked for something harder:
a voice, a presence, a reckoning.
You asked for a book—
like this one.

My name is Shamon Lawrence.
I was enrolled in your teaching poetry course at
Teachers College.
The idea of a chapbook was new to me then.
A way to dabble,
to experiment.

If you remember me,
I was shy at first.
A large Black male presence,
soft-spoken by nature.

I've come to understand this as power.
Your class taught me how to shape it
into presence.

Last summer,
I taught a college writing course.
I invoked your name to explain

how even the essay could carry prophecy.

Essay:
to try.

And in writing these poems,
I tried.

I tried to speak.
I tried to listen.
I tried to enter the tradition
others made room for.

It took time.
Just like your classroom,
I sat quietly before speaking.
I wrestled with your words.
They sharpened me.
Now, my pen is ready
to share its testimony.

This is my first chapbook.
Some people have waited years
to read anything I've written.
But it feels right
that you are reading this first—
or last—
before I close the book.

The title,
The Desk Was Already Here,

is literal.

I inherited a desk.
An actual one.

A bent paper clip.
Tape dangling from a torn corner.
A faint mark that looked like a tear stain.

It felt haunted.
Heavy.
Plagued.
Like it had consumed every person
who dared sit behind it.

I've sat at many desks—
student desks,
sacred desks,
gum-stuck metal frames
and polished wooden pulpits.

Each one holds memory—like RAM, like
rumor, like scripture.
They store up dreams and discipline.
They remember us.

And I hope,
through this book,
you remember me.

Thank you—

for your voice,
your teaching,
your overflow.

I am still learning from it.

I was just supposed to be packing. But some
desks call you back.

—Shamon

Notes on the Poems

The Call
The prologue. This is where I name the tradition, trace the inheritance, and begin the reckoning. Cullen names the tension. Hughes names the method. I answer both.

The Desk Was Already Here
The anchoring poem. The desk is more than furniture—it is altar, archive, surveillance, weight. This was the first piece that made the book inevitable.

The Story Continued
Stillness is not always submission. This poem remembers how even silence had motion, and how sunlight sometimes taught more than the teacher.

The Day Amnesia Swept the School
Celebrated in the morning, erased by afternoon. The poem holds the absurdity of institutional forgetting. It still stings.

The Elephant in the Classroom
There are students I failed. This is for the days I looked away, enforced rules I didn't believe in, or stayed silent when I should have spoken. This letter never left my desk, but it lives here now.

The Desk Is Thirsty
A sinister twist on the desk. It observes, remembers, consumes. Some desks don't just hold memory. They devour it.

"Uncle Law"
A name my students gave me. At first, half joke. Then, something sacred. I never asked for it. But it taught me who I was to them.

Their Desk is Not Our Desk
A reflection on pulpits and pedagogy. I sat in both spaces—church and classroom—and found power in the echoes between them.

Archive Notice
Not everything belongs in the archive. Some of us are still here, still breathing, still teaching. This poem is my refusal to be historicized too soon.

Fire Drill
What would you grab in a fire? I'd reach for the folded notes, the crayon dreams, the kids who trusted me with their stories. The curriculum could burn.

The Bell
It wasn't the sound itself. It was the hush that followed. A moment where 30 children paused and somehow listened back.

"Did You Forget?"
A student asked me this once. Just that. But it followed me home. Some questions haunt not because they're painful, but because they're true.

You Were Already Here
A portrait of a student who never raised their hand, never said much, but taught me presence anyway. Not everyone needs to be called on to be seen.

A Desk Rolls Through New York
Loosely inspired by William Blake's London. I was in a picturesque testing room at NYU, tired, raw, and flooded with light. Somehow, the desk moved, and so did I.

Theme for Writing II
This is my response to Langston Hughes. I took his assignment and wrote it in the classroom where I learned to disappear. But I wrote anyway.

Letter to Countee
A direct address to Cullen. He named the paradox, and I walked it. This letter is part inheritance, part lament, and part offering.

Lemon Loaf
I left a failed final and walked into a Starbucks.
The smell transported me to a nostalgic church
fellowship hall. Sometimes memory saves you
when pride can't.

"Shamon Q. Lawrence"
The nameplate poem. Students fidget with my
desk name, not knowing it holds ghosts. This
poem began as a whisper of a drumbeat. They
never call me Mister.

If You Remember Me
Written to a specific professor, but really to all
who taught me to write, to witness, to respond.
This is the benediction. The final bell.

About the Writer

Shamon Lawrence is a poet, educator, and cultural critic based in New York City. His work explores the sacred and systemic inheritance of classroom spaces, particularly through the lens of Black male educators. The Desk Was Already Here is his debut poetry collection.